Amidst the Rain

Mackenzie Miller

BookLeaf Publishing

Presentation by *BookLeaf Publishing*

Web: www.bookleafpub.com

E-mail: info@bookleafpub.com

ISBN: 9789357440417

First edition 2023

ACKNOWLEDGEMENT

Thank you to my family, best friends, and therapist who have helped me find the light and have never given up on me.

Romanticized Coworkers

Tonight, once the sun
Grabbed its coat &
Shook hands with the moon,
I took the long way home
Just to feel something,
Walking under the scope of
Dim moonlight & the sound
Of recently damp sidewalks.

Shadows comfort my sorrows,
Accepting me & my exhaustion
As one of their own.
We both inhale the bitter air,
Sucking it down like
A stale bottle of wine
Stolen from your mom's garage.
We exhale feelings of nothingness
For the wind to sweep away,
Our frozen destitute lingering
A white cloud, desperate not to
Part our body caverns of cold.

Tonight, during my first
Glance at a life of silence,
I learned about the stars
In the night sky & my

Purpose of existing here
As a figure of glass,
Destined to break
But not shatter.

I recognize now that
When depression visits,
My internal dialogue
Flows like poetry.
Because maybe,
I'm not beautiful
But my words can be.
My adventure gave me
Something to live for
Then took it right back,
When I realized the planets,
The sun & the moon,
Aren't friends nor lovers.
They're just romanticized co-workers.

The Weight of Enough

I'm so heavy.
Why am i so heavy
All of the time?
Every inch of my being
Is dragging against
The sidewalk. My spine
Bends under the pressure
But somehow, my internal
Framework keeps me standing.

My brain suddenly weighs
More than it did before,
One pound too many
For my neck to carry.
My eyelids barely open,
Each blink slower &
Glossier than the last.
My mouth could only
Be pulled into a smile
If people-pleasing &
Faux happiness were
Strings stronger than
The thoughts in my head.
Even my shoulders fall,
Collapsing into my chest

& further strangling my
Heart beat that's trapped
Between deflating lungs.
I'm convinced that maybe
If my legs were to stop
Running & running, chasing
After the people i disappoint,
My skin would melt off
My bones & spread out over
The warm concrete beneath me.

How can i still be heavy,
Even after i've shaved myself
Down to nothing & have
Nothing left to lose?
I guess it's not the heaviness,
It's the tiredness, the exhaustion.
By now i should know,
You can't sleep off the
Weight of never feeling enough.

How to be Unfulfilled

Nobody is truly full-
Only stuffed with ways
To pass the time between
Unavoidable plans &
The gift of going back
To the comfort of sleep.
Each day is simply
Composed of strategies
To make the clock's time
Tick past faster & faster.

Nobody is really whole-
Just filling the gaps &
Emptiness inside them
With something, anything
That makes the suffering
Suck a little bit less.

I would fill myself with
Sand if i could, to keep
Me grounded, feet
Stuck firmly to the ground.
Or maybe i could allow
The everlasting darkness
To prevail. The light only

Attracts nats, bugs
That keep me itching
To run far, far away.

I would fill up on leafy
Branches & yellow flowers
If i thought it would turn
My pain into something beautiful.
The butterflies that once lived
Inside my stomach would return,
The fluttering to make me feel again.
I miss that feeling: excitement.
Or really, the feeling of joy.
Happiness.

Depression is a Paradox

There's an emptiness
Flowing throughout my body
As if i am not built of skin & bones
But a vacant vessel of a person.

At the same time,
I feel full,
Too full.
Every inch of my being stuffed
With the discomfort
Of fear & guilt & sadness.

I guess,
The same is true for the world.
The weight of loneliness rests,
A still burden,
Upon our shoulders.
Yet somehow
When you look around,
This earth contains millions.
You couldn't be alone if you tried.
How strange our brains can be.
Depression is a paradox.

Unrecognizable

It's not my face.
I mean, it is.
It is my face
Painted gray
In the mirror,
Staring back at me
Through vacant eyes
Of green & brown.
It is my mouth,
A thin pressed line
Of emotionless expression.

It is my body,
Standing there
Hunched over & numb,
Not insecure but
Still far from proud.
It is my chest,
Rising & falling with
Each shallow breath.
It is my legs,
Bruised from finding
Ways to feel alive.
It is my hands,

Forever unsettled
As they shake
Against my thighs.

It's not me.
I mean, physically,
It is me. But
I'm not really here.

Sleeping Pill

I cry tears of drowsiness,
A liquid sleeping pill that drops
From my eyes to cheeks & rolls
All the way down past my chin.
Sometimes it's cool to the touch,
Or warm & it stings but a spell
To put me under nonetheless.

My eyelids are too heavy to keep open
Unless tied to the sky by small strings.
They close peacefully,
Not in defeat,
As my breathing slows,
Becoming steady inhales & exhales
In the tempo of my heart beat.
The thoughts in my mind are quiet now
& I don't have the energy to be
suspicious of the voice's whereabouts.
Maybe it's a superpower or
Maybe it's a survival instinct:
The way my brain & body work together
To shut down, protecting me
From the aftermath of
My large storm of feelings.

Daylight Savings

The clocks change,
1 a.m. turns to 3,
Never stopping in order,
Never becoming 2 a.m.
Excluded, shoved aside,
Life walks right past
An empty window
That was once full.

I wish you were 2am.
I wish I could spin a dial
& jump over the timeline of us,
Skip over the tears & the years
& the lies I told myself
To conform my narrative
To match yours.

I wish I wasn't forced
To pause at that measure,
Destroying my cadence
To hum along to yours.

I wish I could fast forward
What came after you.
Because we didn't end

The second I whispered
You weren't good for me
& you begrudgingly
Released your grasp.

I don't wish to erase you.
By erasing what happened to us,
What happened to me,
I'd be deleting my present self
Like the thousands of texts
I have never sent.

I just wish I could
Shorten the duration
Of my grievance of you,
Of the person I was
Before you broke me
When I already needed fixing.

Someday, you'll be my 2 a.m.
I'll step out my door,
Inhale the present,
& turn to face the future.
I won't forget you exist.
I won't be mad or
Sad about it anymore.
I'll just be me
& I'll be okay.

The Day You Left

Laying on my back
Staring at the ceiling fan
Spin round & round in
The same counterclockwise
Circle it's moved in for years.

Blurry vision but this time
It's not from the tears
Flowing down my cheeks,
Like the vignette of an
Old fashioned photograph,
The darkness creeps in
From all sides & angles.
The mint green walls gray
As if I've laid here simply
Observing it age.

Objects become shapes,
Become abstract, become
Nothing but a fluid configuration
Of colors, moving in & out of each
Other, unsure of a final form to take.

I blink to clear my vision,
Hoping my tears will wipe away
The colorless room around me
Like a windshield wiper
On a car window.
It doesn't bring clarity,
Just smudges the horizon.

My eyelids feel heavy
But can't easily shut.
My blinks slow then stop;
My lungs unhurried to fill with air.
No more liquid falls from my eyes
& the remnants dry on my skin,
Burning & stinging my face.

It's too difficult to move,
So here I stay in my cave
Of abstract nonsense,
Hoping if you return to me,
The color will come back.

Butterflies

You give me butterflies in my stomach.
No, not butterflies, knots.
Slowly, you learned to control me,
Like a puppet, pulling strings from the inside.

In the past, you pulled hard enough
To form smaller messes that
Tied together in one large clump
At the bottom of my stomach.
For a while, they held taut.
Each time I thought of you,
They tightened around my organs,
Snaking up my lungs to prevent my breathing.
There I sat, consumed by that pain,
Patiently waiting for someone to come
Untangle the mess you created.
I don't feel the knots anymore,
At least, not like I used to anyways.
Sometimes, I feel uneasy thinking
About the ways you took advantage
Of me, of my vulnerability.
The knots don't strangle me
When your voice replays in my mind now
Because someone, after all of this time,
Cut the strings. Cut me free.

Sometimes I wonder if you ever
Feel knots in your stomach when
You think about me.
Do you become nauseous as you
Contemplate why you tortured me?
Or do you not have to live with the
Consequences of your actions
Like I had to?

Either way, I am not your puppet.
The strings have been cut.
The ties have been severed.
You couldn't control me now
Even if you wanted to.

Healing

I am worth more than
All of the bad things
That you said about me.
I am worth more than
The seven vowels &
Eight consonants
When you said
I was worthless.

No matter how hard
My brain tries to argue,
A fact cannot be changed
Based on your opinion of me.

Thunderstorms

Thunderstorms compare,
Oh so wonderfully,
To an explosion of feelings.
The rain so soft
Feels as though a tear
Gracefully slides down our cheek.
A heavy downpour;
The signifying sobs
Of too much weight.
The thunderous claps
Increase as they grow
Stronger & stronger,
Closer & closer to the end.
Only when the clouds are light,
Freed of their sorrows,
Do we feel the relief
Of clearer skies coming.
If only we could learn
to appreciate each other
As we do the weather.

No Control

My mind is split in two
The dark side winning the war.
I can't promise you anything,
Safety contracts or pinky swears,
Because just like you,
I, too, have no control.
No mental reigns to harness the
Wild, destructive actions
Of prolonged diet culture.
How peculiar it is
That a desperate search for control
Resulted in losing more.

Problem

Please don't call me difficult,
Shrugging off the efforts I fight to give you,
Even if they don't appear on a chart
As the results you pleaded for.
Please don't say I am resistant;
I fight hourly battles within my own body
& conquer villains in my head by the minute.
Please don't look only at my symptoms,
Wrapping my fragile brain
In heavy duty duct tape
& sending me out in confident
Declaration that you "fixed" me.
Please don't separate yourself from me,
Just because I am struggling to survive
Does not mean I am a problem
Any more than I am a person.

Sick Enough

The truth is you'll never feel sick enough.
not when your hair thins & falls,
not when your bones show & ache,
not when your heart falters & stops.

The truth is you'll never feel sick enough.
not when you can't sit up in bed,
not when you don't recognize your reflection,
not when you are convinced this time
it will actually be the last time.

The truth is you'll never feel sick enough.
not when you lie to loved ones,
not when you shake in summer heat,
not when you're scared to fall asleep
at the very possible chance
you won't wake up the next morning.

The truth is you were sick enough
the moment you looked in the mirror
& decided you weren't good enough.

Letter to my Eating Disorder

When will it be enough?
The efforts I make to heal & recover
Or give in & lose everything
I have worked for.
Nothing will ever be enough for you.
Why can't I be enough for you?

It's all I have wanted for 8 years now.
When will you let me go?
How many more years must i live
With you in control of
Every move I make,
Thought i think,
& food I don't eat?
I thought I was in control.
All along, you were tricking me
For your own enjoyment.

Aren't you bored yet?
Aren't you tired?
Cause I am.
Tired of memorizing
The calories in my vitamins
Or the number of steps to
Burn off my own birthday cake.

Haven't you caused enough damage?
I will never be the same.

My body will never be the same.
Unable to digest nutrients
Or regulate my hormones
Or trust my heart
To function reliably.

I'll never look at the world the same.
Other people are a vessel for comparison,
That show me what I don't have
& what I need to lose.
A scale isn't a measure of gravity,
But a measure of my worth.

You have ruined me.
Poisoned me.
I will never be able to return
The thoughts you handed me
Like a contract I signed
But cannot break.
A deal that keeps me alive
But makes me wish I wasn't.

I don't know how to live without you.
But I will not die with you.
I refuse to let you kill me.
I refuse to let you win.
You're stubborn, but I am too.

I used to think that
It would be so much better
If I were dead.
Now I know that isn't true.

It would be so much better if you were.
The part of me that is you
Is free to go.
You are not all that I am
& I am sick of being unable
To tell the difference some days.

I did not choose you.
I did not do this to myself.
I refuse to let you convince me
That I signed myself up for this.
You gave the pen to a child.
I was only 10.
I didn't know any better.
She didn't know any better.
She couldn't distinguish
Her voice from yours.
But I can.
Your voice is not welcome
In my head anymore.
You cannot live here,
Feasting on my insecurities.
I am finished allowing you
To ruin me.
I am done letting you
Steal my life from me.

May 27th

May 27th
The morning after I was discharged
From the psych ward.
A text sent to a friend:
I woke up this morning & for the first time,
I didn't feel angry to be alive.

Not every morning feels like this.
I would be lying if I said most do.
It's an agonizing thing to do,
To open your eyes & think
I can't do this again.
But sometimes there is hope,
Scattered between the nights
You can barely hold on &
Waking up on mornings
Just wishing that you didn't.
One day you will inhale &
It won't feel so heavy.

Letter to my Brain

Dear brain,
Please stop bullying my body.
I recognize your anxiety in
Feeling full instead of hungry
& guilt for eating the food you
Fought as an adversary for years.
Please do not punish her with
Exercise or ruminate on what
You perceive as her flaws.
She's already tired & in need of rest.
I acknowledge your feelings & fears;
We'll work through them together.
Please remember my body is
My home & not my enemy.
She doesn't need to feel ashamed
For behaving or looking as she pleases.
She deserves so much more love.
Please stop bullying my body.

Progress

Last month i denied my
Body rest from our fighting,
Punishing her for delivering
The message of my hunger
& existing naturally as she is..

Yesterday i woke up in the
Late morning & took a deep breath,
Nourishing my lungs & my spirit.
My mind told me to get up,
Do something, be something,
But i knew i was purposefully
Leaving someone out
As if her needs didn't matter.
I asked her, my body,
What she needed, what she wanted.
& she told me she needed rest.
She wanted to stay in bed longer.
So for the first time,
I listened & i thought
Okay, we'll rest.

Sometimes our brains need a sick day.
Sometimes our bodies need a vacation.
Sometimes, all we need is for someone
To hold us & listen to our cries &
Tell us we are okay to only exist.
Sometimes, our progress surprises us.

Why

When we discuss
Eating disorder recovery,
We highlight the big things.
They talk up weight restoration
& things we pretend to care about.

They don't feature
The importance of motivation.
How necessary the "why" is.
Recovery isn't all rainbows,
But it isn't all storm clouds either.
It's the most crucial trust exercise
In your life, balancing the highs
& lows in your mind body relationship.
You have to learn who you are:
Whether or not to trust that
Incessant, nagging voice in your head.
Because when it comes,
& it will come,
You have to know how to fight back.
How to not let a longing for control
& the influence of death steal your voice.
It can't take your why
If you believe enough in it.

The Moon

You know that feeling,
When it's 2 a.m.,
& you're the only person awake?
When you can finally inhale deep
Enough to satisfy your lungs
& your thoughts quiet,
Listening to the sweet
Stillness of the world?
When you feel so vulnerable
Yet completely loved
At the same time?
The moon is stretching
Her soft arms down to you,
Embracing you in the darkness.

The Beauty of Complexity

I often worry that I am not enough.
But other times, I feel that I am all too much.
It's a strange & confusing concept
When you think about it.
How can I believe something
So strongly one minute,
Then contradict myself the next?
Bouncing between realities where in one,
I will never be worthy of the love & attention
I am receiving,
While in the other,
I need to tone myself down &
Turn into someone I am not.

When I think about it in one way,
It's harmful & Sends me spiraling
Down an endless tunnel,
Where I don't know who I am,
Who I want to be,
Or who I should be.

But in another sense, It is beautiful.
It is beautiful how complex & chaotic humans truly
are.
It is beautiful how we can feel, sense, breathe, act,
& experience moments one way,
Then contradict ourselves in a secondary manner;
Our minds pointing arrows,

Going a hundred different directions at once.
It is beautiful how many things can be true at the
same time;
How we can be many things at once.

As humans, we are not limited.
We are not restricted to one size, one color, one
shape, one mold.
We are not meant to fit as a puzzle piece in a binary
system,
Where we must be this or that,
But in a world where we are everything in between.

Despite how complex & chaotic we are,
I think our purpose is to just be.
& that is a beautiful thing;
To know that whoever you are,
Whoever you want to be, or
Whoever you feel you should be,
Is enough.

Printed in the USA
CPSIA information can be obtained
at www.ICGtesting.com
LVHW021552211223
766988LV00097B/5703

9 789357 440417